To:_____

_____
From:_____

FoR You,
Mom

Published by Sellers Publishing, Inc.
161 John Roberts Road, South Portland, ME 04106
Visit us at www.sellerspublishing.com • E-mail: rsp@rsvp.com

Compiled by Robin Haywood.

ISBN-13: 978-1-4162-4545-2

Printed and bound in China.

10 9 8 7 6 5 4 3 2 1

FoR You, Mom

Art & Design by **ROBIN PICKENS**
Compiled by **ROBIN HAYWOOD**

SELLERS
PUBLISHING

I stand up a bit taller
when someone tells
me that I'm just
like my mother.

—AUTHOR UNKNOWN

Proud

Sanctuary

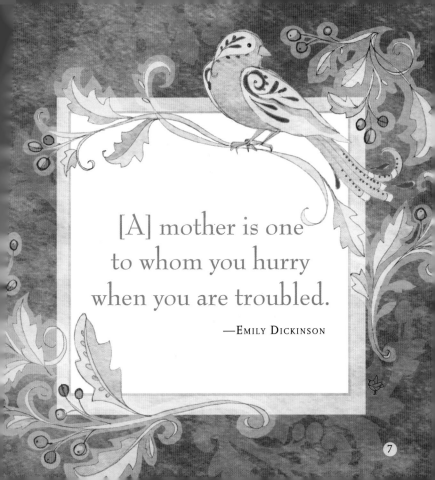

[A] mother is one
to whom you hurry
when you are troubled.

—Emily Dickinson

The heart of a mother
is a deep abyss at
the bottom of which
you will always find
forgiveness.

—HONORÉ DE BALZAC

Compassion

Love

There's nothing
like a mama-hug.

—TERRI GUILLEMETS

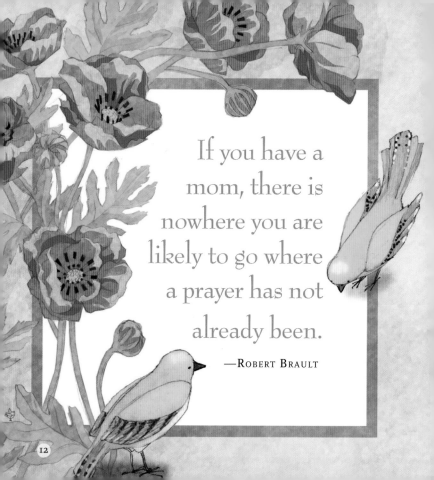

If you have a
mom, there is
nowhere you are
likely to go where
a prayer has not
already been.

—ROBERT BRAULT

12

Protect

13

Devotion

No language can
express the power,
and beauty, and
heroism, and majesty
of a mother's love.

—EDWIN HUBBELL CHAPIN

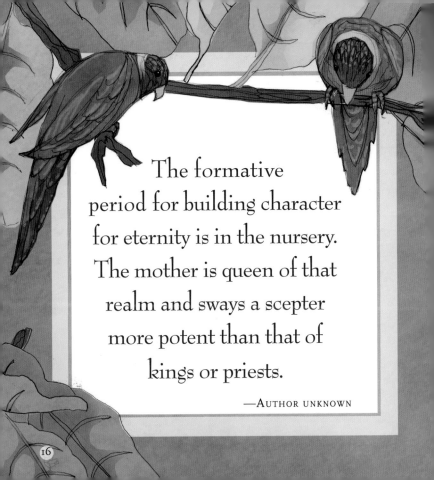

The formative
period for building character
for eternity is in the nursery.
The mother is queen of that
realm and sways a scepter
more potent than that of
kings or priests.

—AUTHOR UNKNOWN

Nurture

Happiness

Don't ever tell
the mother of a
newborn that
her baby's smile
is just gas.

—Jill Woodhull

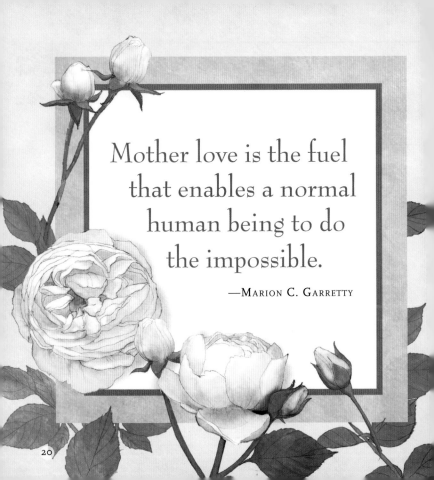

Mother love is the fuel that enables a normal human being to do the impossible.

—Marion C. Garretty

Extraordinary

Lapse

A Freudian slip is
when you say one
thing but mean
your mother.

—AUTHOR UNKNOWN

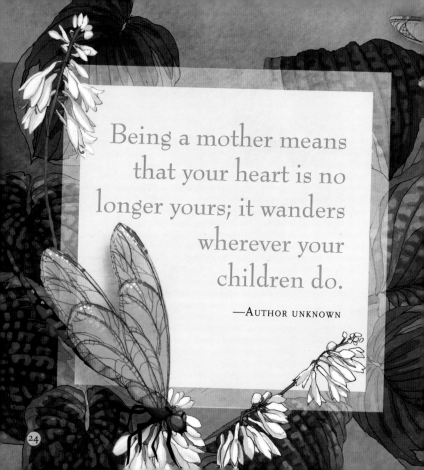

Being a mother means
that your heart is no
longer yours; it wanders
wherever your
children do.

—AUTHOR UNKNOWN

Guardian

Responsibility

When you are a mother,
you are never really alone
in your thoughts. A mother
always has to think twice,
once for herself and once
for her child.

—SOPHIA LOREN

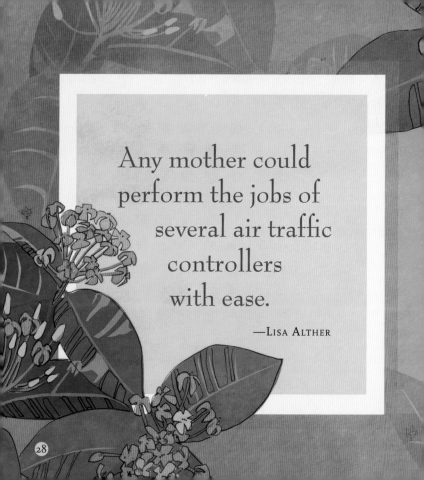

Any mother could perform the jobs of several air traffic controllers with ease.

—LISA ALTHER

Attentive

Energetic

If evolution really
works, how come
mothers only have
two hands?

—MILTON BERLE

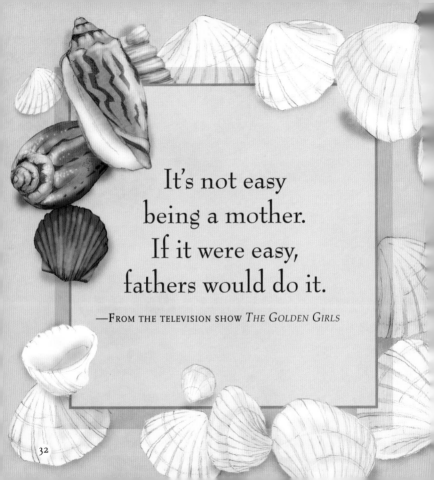

It's not easy
being a mother.
If it were easy,
fathers would do it.

—FROM THE TELEVISION SHOW *THE GOLDEN GIRLS*

Formidable

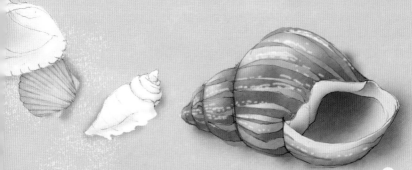

A mother is the truest friend we have, when trials heavy and sudden fall upon us; when adversity takes the place of prosperity; when friends who rejoice with us in our sunshine desert us; when trouble thickens around us, still will she cling to us, and endeavor by her kind precepts and counsels to dissipate the clouds of darkness, and cause peace to return to our hearts.

—WASHINGTON IRVING

Faithful

Character

Some mothers are kissing
mothers and some are
scolding mothers, but
it is love just the
same, and most
mothers kiss and
scold together.

—PEARL S. BUCK

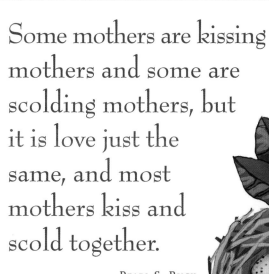

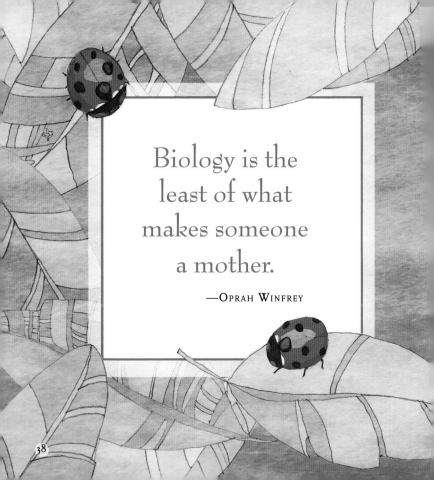

Biology is the
least of what
makes someone
a mother.

—OPRAH WINFREY

Parent

Destiny

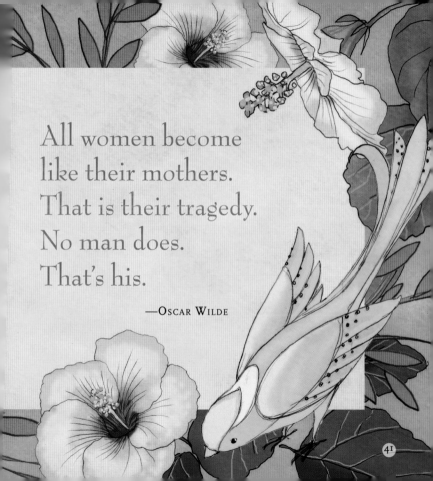

All women become
like their mothers.
That is their tragedy.
No man does.
That's his.

—Oscar Wilde

Sweater, n.: garment
worn by a child when its
mother is feeling chilly.

—AMBROSE BIERCE

Concern

Dedication

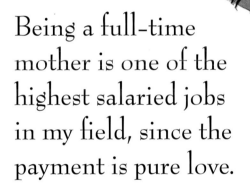

Being a full-time mother is one of the highest salaried jobs in my field, since the payment is pure love.

—MILDRED B. VERMONT

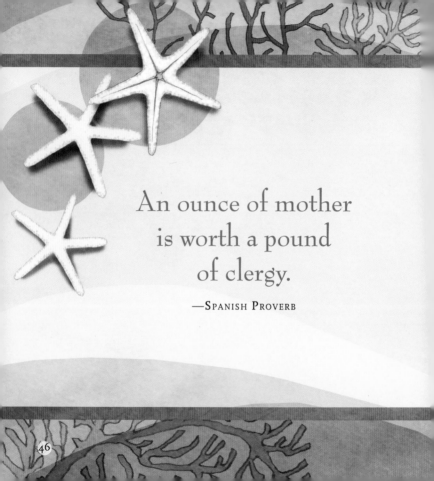

An ounce of mother
is worth a pound
of clergy.

—SPANISH PROVERB

Appreciate

Big-hearted

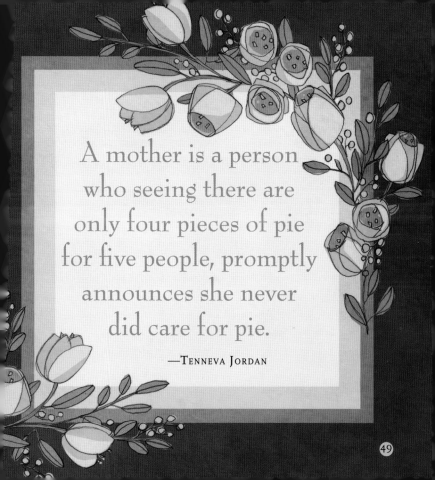

A mother is a person
who seeing there are
only four pieces of pie
for five people, promptly
announces she never
did care for pie.

—Tenneva Jordan

49

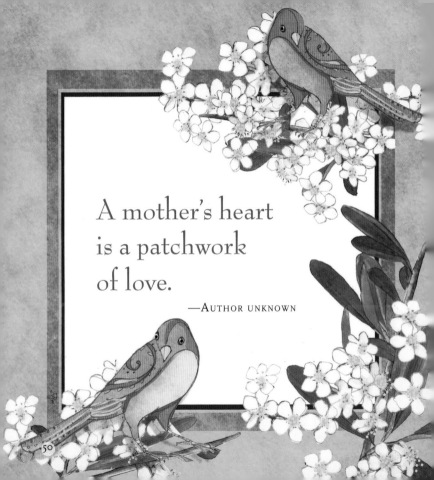

A mother's heart
is a patchwork
of love.

—AUTHOR UNKNOWN

Soul

Mother

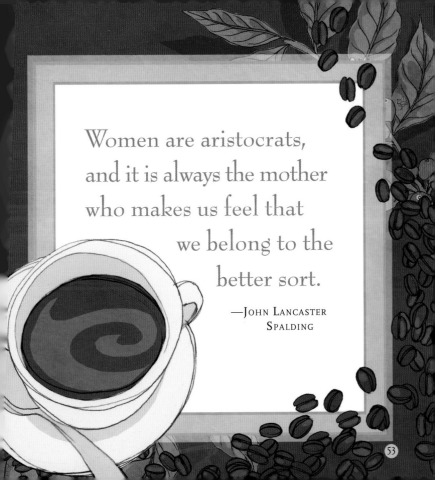

Women are aristocrats, and it is always the mother who makes us feel that we belong to the better sort.

—JOHN LANCASTER SPALDING

She never quite leaves
her children at home,
even when she doesn't
take them along.

—MARGARET CULKIN BANNING

Heartfelt

Spirit

The real religion of
the world comes from
the world comes from
women much more
than from men — from
mothers most of all, who
carry the key of our souls
in their bosoms.

—OLIVER WENDELL HOLMES

Motherhood has
a very humanizing effect.
Everything gets reduced
to essentials.

—MERYL STREEP

Necessary

Duty

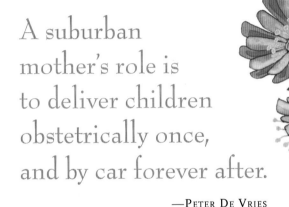

A suburban
mother's role is
to deliver children
obstetrically once,
and by car forever after.

—PETER DE VRIES

All I am
I owe to
my mother.

—GEORGE WASHINGTON

Gratitude

CREDITS

p. 20 Marion C. Garretty, from *A Little Spoonful of Chicken Soup for the Mother's Soul, Garborg's Heart 'n' Home, 1999*, William Morrow and Co., 1984; p. 27 Sophia Loren, *Women and Beauty* p. 32 from the television show *The Golden Girls*; p. 41 Oscar Wilde, *The Importance of Being Earnest, 1895*